train

CA 37

ISBN 978-1-4768-0854-3

HAL•LEONARD® CORPORATION
7777 W. BLUEMOUND RD. P.O. BOX 13819 MILWAUKEE, WI 53213

In Australia Contact:
Hal Leonard Australia Pty. Ltd.
4 Lentara Court
Cheltenham, Victoria, 3192 Australia
Email: ausadmin@halleonard.com.au

Visit Hal Leonard Online at
www.halleonard.com

THIS'LL BE MY YEAR

Words and Music by PAT MONAHAN,
BUTCH WALKER, DAVE KATZ
and SAM HOLLANDER

Moderate Rock beat

In Eigh-ty Five, __ Tues-day morn-in' came a-live, I did-n't know __ ya.

Route Six-ty Six __ is gone, __ Rea-gan's here, __ it won't __ be long. __ Nin-

ten-do comes, Live __ Aid too. Back __ To The Fu-ture, where __ were you? __ Well,

I spent all ___ my days ___ in Cath - 'lic school. In

Eigh - ty Nine ___ the dream ___ be - gins, ___ first in line to Cal - i - for - nia.

Pete Rose is banned for good, the Simp - sons come to Hol - ly - wood. ___

Rus - sia leaves ___ Af - ghan - i - stan, ___ flight 1 0 3 ___ ends ___ Pan Am.

called it a day. ___ May - be this-'ll be my year. ___

May - be this-'ll be my year. ___

May - be this-'ll be my year. ___

To Coda ⊕

May - be this-'ll be my year. ___

D.S. al Coda

leaves San - Fran - cis - co in a thou - sand dol - lar van.

CODA

Two Thou-sand One the tow - ers fell, __ the

world is stunned, I wish I knew ya. I was on __ a plane, __ the

world would nev - er be the same. The ar - ti - fi - cial heart is born, __ how i -

DRIVE BY

Words and Music by PAT MONAHAN,
ESPEN LIND and AMUND BJORKLAND

FEELS GOOD AT FIRST

Words and Music by PAT MONAHAN
and ALLEN SHAMBLIN

Teach me to fall___ and I'll

teach you to sing___ when life keeps steal - in'___ your mel - o - dy. A-

round your fin - ger___ I'll be a string.___ I will for - get___

Na, na, na, na, na, na, na, na, na, na, na,

Csus2   G/B   Dsus/A   G5

umm. _____   Na, na, na, na, na, na,

Csus2   G/B   Dsus/A   G5

na, na, na, na, na, umm _____

D/F#   D   G

___   but it sure felt good ___ at first. ___

BRUISES

Words and Music by PAT MONAHAN,
ESPEN LIND and AMUND BJORKLUND

Male: Have - n't seen you __ since __ high school. __

Good to see you're still __ beau - ti - ful. __

Grav - i - ty has - n't start - ed __ to pull quite

D.S. al Coda

Male: Leav - in' you makes me ___ wan - na cry. ___ *Both:* These

CODA

Male: I would love to fix it all for ___ you. ___

Female: I would love to fix you ___ too. ___

Both: Please don't fix a thing what - ev - er you do. ___

50 WAYS TO SAY GOODBYE

Words and Music by PAT MONAHAN,
ESPEN LIND and AMUND BJORKLUND

Recorded a half step lower.

I wan-na live a thou-sand lives____ with you.____ I wan-

YOU CAN FINALLY MEET MY MOM

Words and Music by PAT MONAHAN
and JERRY T. BECKER

Don't cry when I die. When it's my time I pro-'bly won't die, I'll just lie down and close my eyes and think a-bout stuff. These eyes got too wise, seen too much of life's good-byes.

* Recorded a half step lower.

SING TOGETHER

Words and Music by PAT MONAHAN,
ESPEN LIND and AMUND BJORKLUND

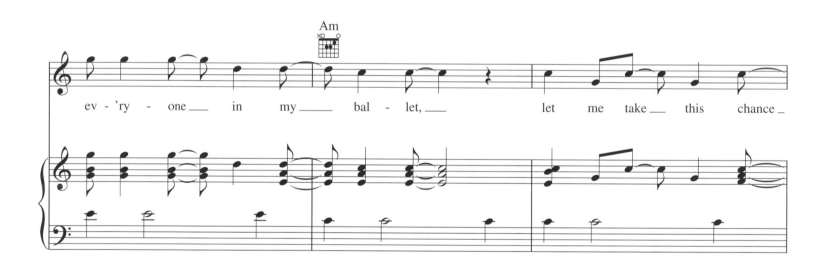

* Recorded a half step higher.

MERMAID

Words and Music by PAT MONAHAN,
ESPEN LIND, AMUND BJORKLUND,
TOR HERMANSEN and MIKKEL ERIKSEN

CALIFORNIA 37

Words and Music by PAT MONAHAN,
GREG WATTENBERG and DIJI PARQ

* *Recorded a half step higher.*

WE WERE MADE FOR THIS

Words and Music by PAT MONAHAN
and BUTCH WALKER

Love and star-dust set-tle on __ us like a net, while Buck-ley's "Hal-le-lu-jah" fills our ears __ __ from your __ cas-sette, __ while my heart stops beat-ing, and you stop breath-ing, Ju-li-et. __

You're the on - ly thing I'm ev - er gon - na miss,

oh, but we were made for this.

Repeat and Fade | **Optional Ending**

WHEN THE FOG ROLLS IN

Words and Music by PAT MONAHAN
and GREG WATTENBERG

go - ing up ___ for sale. The fog kept on

roll - ing in; ___ the time came to sink ___ or swim. They say it's bet - ter ___

___ to try and fail, ___ and we tried ___ like ___

___ hell. ___

I take a deep ___ breath with my hand on the door, ___ a - fraid 'cause I'm ___ not gon - na see ___ you an - y -